A Light from a Son

K.A. Smith

A Light from a Son

A Light from a Son

Waiting there in the gaps is a beast
With teeth.
Bravery afraid to... enter.

It's in clothing
Between moldings.
It's protected from a distance.

Too, it's me.
I filled the gaps against.
Get!

Rubbed...
Every time, love.
A being, attractive being.
Open...
Nice dream.

Freed words.
Out, sings like a bird.
Rest, never heard.

Here...
Early this morning, dear.
I rung, because
Near.
Give reason for being.

The one I love, a rose.
More than a hug,
Deeper in my soul.
A powerful feeling, my...
Charm with a face.
Heart locked, unfolds.
The one I love...
Have told.

Belle...
Can't afford happiness,
But I can afford rest
And will dream of
Moving mountains and
Flying through space
Though.

SPECIAL TIMES

Looked at my hand...
Special times.
It's a point to land.

STAYED HOME

Wrote a poem.
A ode to her.
"Do not disturb."

"Set" and "Ready"
Anticipated beyond peeks.
The juice,
Laughed from proof.

Love for the game,
"Set" and "Ready"
Stayed home.

HONEY!

Runny...
A bug passed to me.
A teddy bear bee,
Made.
It's so warm.
Honey, please.
An old sipping...
Me, thank you.
"Honey!"

PRAISE

Gazed...
"A cape saved."
Thanks for the guide, the breast is alive.
My horizon, wide.

Thanks received in waves,
Problem no more.
Whenever I look up, he or she.

Raise
By the show of hands,
You are, You are...Praised.

Blinded by the light,
Climbs.
'Cause of lonely,
Not homey.

A cast
Appeared upon her face.
She fell in love.
Flight, talking with grace.

"Love is blind."
All that matters.

SQUEEZE

The sadness is contagious.
Crimes are neighbors.
Riding to lines...
The finish, that's mine.
Behavior is living.
Inside, live.
Always at the door.

Don't mind anymore.
The pressure usually be
Before, Mr. Happy.
Leave, sit,... squeeze.

WONDER

Wonder...
My home on my own land.
Does it feel like my bare hands.
My own imagination off paper.
Will it be?
Yes! My imagination.

Wonder...
If the door reached the sky.
Possible...
Grants the wish to fly.

Big deal to some people who rent.
Big deal for those comfortable in a "compartment."
For the sake of "Art-meant."

Living in "As is" or "Is as" sounds fun.
Work and enjoyment when it's done.
With all this...
On my own.
Won...

A Boy!
A bundle, a joy.
Like wind, love is in.

Looking,
A moment so warm.
People took and hooked like a storm
For thoughts.
Don't mind?
It's real and fine.

Emotion is hard to help
With tears in sight.
Cried within
For a little boy.
Fight!

I need to see.
Thirst...
This has been.

To me, Happy birthday!
The first.

SOMEBODY

Carts in the turning lane,
And false starts.
Because of hearts,
Traffic has slowed.
For somebody,
It's a blessing.
Gold, no matter the blame.

Have gained,
Because somebody changed.

WISH

A wish to be
For what's to come in a surprise.
When!
Be wise.
Have patience inside.

BEETS UP

"Pull seat up,"
Pulled.
What's to eat?
Chicken, rice, carrots, and
Beets.

I looked down mad.
Of all things to cook, it's for my friend,
Glad.

He liked them so,
for show.
Protested glad.
Beets up.

They're there!
Everywhere,
Swarming.
Of glares, rare.

Golden beetles
In her hair.
Go to a place.
Where?

There?
Did they come
From a treat?
Where she felt bum.

Was it the scarab
With her and friends?
Sparkling on a hill.
The end.

BULLY-LESS

Bully-less and hooommmee free.
A child doesn't like to give away
The prize from family.
From breakfast to dinner,
Feels like a winner.

Get a load!
It's the new kid stepping out.
Of the room, Gold!
A cloud with a silver lining,
The parent analyzed "Poor baby."
Outside is tiny.

Sees his or her boundary
Without explaining here.
"Don't you ever ever come near!"

For whoever limits a prosperous journey.
Slows a child's learny.
A short ride forever is not fun
For a daughter
Or a son.

EFFECTIVENESS

Nothing is more effective than light.
It impacts everything,
And it's strong like a bite. It unites.

Can't fight the body as a whole.
It has included without cold.
It grows with love.

Effectively providing safety and comfort,
Relaxed by the bulb.

Rest...
Know it stays on at night.
Morning is fast.
Sleep tight.

A HOOP

Why?
A hoop, buy.
To pattern myself.
To recognize
Inside and outside.

BE GOOD

Keep it in.
In and confined.
Be disciplined.
Be good.
Be kind.
Move however you want.
Keep the monster in line.
In the sun.
For he/she has a monster
Inside it sits,
Locked
Until picked.
Don't be remembered
For throwing sticks.
Be good.

UMBRELLA

A job,
Like an umbrella.
Then can buy.
It would rain no more
In someone's eyes.

Tomorrow,
A wet day born...
So dance!
No slips!
No frets!
No horns!

Amazing days like these are prey.
A beautiful sky in every way.
For sewing clouds,
Pay.

IT'S WEATHER

It's weather,
When enough.
A cuff,
A fold.
Warm or cold.
Leaves an opening...
A thought in
Nature is rough.

THUMBS UP!

Thumbs up!
Raise them high!
As high as they can go!
Cheers from my best man
Belted words loudly
And drunkenly slow.

I wouldn't haven't any.
Other ways I pay.
Dessert treats me well.
I want to avoid the wine
And the glass bells.

From my best man,
"Thumbs up!"
What?!!
I don't mind.
He's the life.
It's love.

HAVE FUN!

Have fun!
Don't waste it.
Life
Is only
Won.
Don't shun the one
Who tries to rain
On the sun.

A special kind.
Yes!
It's all mine.
A crooked neck.
Strange in the rind,
And smiles a lot.

What the heck?!!
Yes!

Never was
About the dulls.
It's kindness
That sends me above.

A club with three eyes?
It'll look funny.
There'd be people circling
In the ring.
A lead will shout, "Enjoy their strange."
"The inheritance!"
It looks unique, strangely, and famely
In the roots. "Experience it!"
Somewhere hiding in the bleak,
They're shy and afraid to come outside.
Show it.
I'm able to relate.
I'd put on my costume
And have at it.
A masquerade party if you will.
Then afterward we are all
Chill.

MEOWEEEY

Meoweey...
It's an itty-bitty kittie
Following its do-diddie.
It mimics thee,
And fell-ee
In a watery sea.
Oweeey.

DIRTY GLASSES

Dirty glasses, can't see.
Now, 1...
Folding my neck,
Feels like cloth, not free.

Frames like iron on my nose.
Lenses, hot.
Fogs up from winter's cold.

Blind, covered in silk.
Flakes are even more defined, like milk.
Red, hopefully,
If someone crosses my path.
A stop sign in a language
On the dash.

DISPLAYS

Display chalk!
Reveal its faults.
For a full moon frets,
And stims.
Why choose a desk?
Why!

THE FRUIT FLY

The fruit fly
Searches for dew nearby.
Like bees to honey,
It orders
Dinner and dessert on the fly.

It's homescape,
As wide as the eye can see.
To it, a prepared feast.

WHAT TIME CURTAIN TIME IS?

What time curtain time is?
Anticipating comfort and
Going there
Where dreams live.

Don't clap, or I'll begin
Moving while sleep,
Immersed in the deep.
Shouts of "Encore! Encore!"
Clap! Clap! wakes up.
Wait 'til the end.

THE TALE OF THE APPLE SEEDS

There's a farmer resting on a tree
After tending to an orchard full of apples tirelessly.
Eyes gazing at the horizon, the farmer didn't notice
The passing of time,
So he decided to end the break
And scour for seeds on the ground.
The farmer landed on seeds
His eyes couldn't believe.
He planted them, then went home to sleep.
The next morning, he woke up to apples adorning.
The farmer asked strange beings, "Why did this happen to
me?"
They replied with "Look for the seeds. Good journeys!"
The farmer did what they told him.
The search was golden.
The seeds took the farmer back to reality,
And wishing for another adventurous dream.
The next day, he looked hard and tirelessly
For the same apple seeds.

DIAMONDS IN RHYTHM

There's a diamond hiding
Underneath
With joy,
So attractive,
So active,
A youth I wish for,
And adore.

There's a diamond hiding
In my hand.
Invite me in.
How do I begin?
Oh boy!
The wind is blowing,
So attractive,
So active,
The eye..
Cannot avoid.

A glimmer
For all to witness.
The constant burst,
The diamond in rhythm,
Celebrating the day coal crumbled,
And revealing
Her.

If could stay this way.
A good husband and father,
A good wife and mother,
A good man,
A good woman,
A good leader and guardian.
If could stay this way,
It is okay.
It is...

A way.

Dedication

To all the loved ones.

A Light from a Son

The End

www.ingramcontent.com/pod-product-compliance
Lightning Source LLC
Chambersburg PA
CBHW071237140726
47996CB00007B/2642